A PURPOSE-FILLED DASH
Living an Empire State of Mind

Cheryl Barton

Dedication

I dedicate this book to my mother, Barbara, the most incredible woman I know. Your love and support of me has helped me know, love and appreciate who I am and that I should live a happy life filled with purpose. To my biggest supporter, my mother, I salute you and I thank God for you.

Dedications

About A Purpose-Filled Dash

A Purpose-Filled Dash is how I see my life, full of opportunity and purpose.

My purpose-filled dash is the time I'm given every day to rise and make every moment count. To make that happen, each day I say or write something to myself to reflect on so that I don't forget how precious life is and how important it is to speak life not only to myself and over my circumstances, but into the lives of others.

This is my story on the dash.

Live a Dream and Build a Dynasty

Dreams of a better life are real. They are promises that though you may feel down or bound, it won't last forever if you take that first step toward making a dream a reality.

Not everyone started out at the top. Some started at the bottom and they erected a ladder that enabled them to climbed toward a dream that others may have thought impossible. They had hope that though they may not get there today or even tomorrow, as long as they keep that dream alive and work toward it, they could do more than imagine how big of a dynasty they could build.

Don't just dream a dream, but live in that dream and imagine the higher heights it could take you to.

Empowering Self-Confidence

If you find my confidence, power and determination overpowering or intimidating, don't back away; join me in embracing the greatness of the king or queen that God birthed in you just as He did in me. I feel empowered to do my best, be my best and live my best and I can only do that if I am sure of the greatness that is already within me.

Live Without Apologies

I live my life without apologies, loving the space and the skin I'm in. My confidence enters a room before I do because I know that my steps have been ordered and I proudly walk in them where the vision has been written and made clear for me to see and follow. I choose to not doubt what is my destiny.

A Lidless Jar

I'm thankful for every conversation I have because each provides an opportunity for me to learn something. During a recent conversation, the comment was made to me by someone who said, "I thought you were a romance novelist, but I see you also write inspirational works as well." My response to that statement was, "I consider myself a writer and I don't limit what genre I will write."

That conversation had me thinking of a jar with a lid. The jar with the lid symbolizes the limits we place on what we can do. I'm a person who is a jar that has no lid. I never want to think that I was blessed with a talent and I'm only seeing it as one-dimensional. I believe as a writer, I should explore writing whatever is in my heart to write.

When I'm writing, I am a lidless jar because I

have plans to write not only romance and inspirational works, but mystery, sci-fi or whatever other genre is placed in my spirit to write about.

That lidless jar applies to everything in life. Why limit yourself because someone else thinks that's all there is to you. Make sure the jar that you are has no lid and explore every opportunity that comes your way. You'll never know what you can be if you see a path that has an end. Release the lid that's holding you back and free yourself. It will be life-changing.

Words Can Hurt

There are some things that you're thinking that should be left as a thought and never be spoken. Once words that are meant to hurt in the heat of anger are out there, even an apology can't take them back. They will spread like a virus to kill and destroy. Consider writing down what you're feeling and reading them back to yourself, pondering your reaction if it were said to you. If those words seem harsh and you're insulted, someone else would be too.

Shine a Light

Encourage someone's creative ability today so that we can admire their creative genius tomorrow.

A Brand New Day

Don't give up the fight today because tomorrow comes with the prospect of something brand new. Imagine getting through the darkness of the night before and to wake up to the bright sunshine of a brand new day ready for you to make a positive change that you were unable to do the day before.

You're Tougher Than You Think

Women can go through the pain of childbirth, remember the pain and then do it again and again.

I remember that pain and if I ever thought I was weak before, childbirth gave me a new outlook on how to deal with challenges as they come along. I knew that if I could handle that, I can handle anything.

Come on hurdle because I'm ready to climb over you!

Flaws Don't Define You

Don't seek validation in other people's opinions of you; they are flawed just like you and the difference between you and them could be whether you digress or progress.

Women Are Daughters

Men, take a look at your daughters and think about how you want a man to approach her and treat her when she begins dating. Use that as an example for how you approach and treat a woman. After all, that woman is someone's daughter too.

Lighten Up

Some people are wound way too tight on a regular basis. Each day when they wake up, they need to take an extra nap, learn to lighten up and appreciate each and every breath and not look at everything that is meant to help you put a smile on your face and find everything wrong with it. Try looking at the glass as half full and see how much brighter your day could be.

Lend a Hand

When you see someone struggling with a step you've already taken, reach back and lend a helping hand especially if someone did that for you.

A Clean House

Unleash the clutter of people, places and things in your life and watch God fill it will peace, love and happiness.

No Compromise

Don't compromise your craft; be the exception to those who do by following your dream and never giving up. After you reach the top, you don't want to second guess the choices you had to make to get there.

Steamed Crabs Makes Everything Better

Nothing relaxes me like sitting at a table full of Maryland steamed crabs. I believe everyone has something that they love and no matter how bad things are, that something makes everything better. When you're feeling stressed and need to unwind, grab hold of your that something and jump in feet first. Sometimes all it takes to make everything right in the world is to enjoy something that wipes all of your woes away.

I've noticed that my friends know me just as well as I know myself. When I'm speaking with them and I'm having a bad day, their first recommendation is to have girl talk over a table full of crabs.

There's nothing wrong with indulging in the simpler things in life that make you happy and when you have friends who share the same loves, grab up a few, relax in your most comfortable attire and get your eat on and for me, crabs have never, ever failed me.

Lead or Be Led

Leaders lead from the front, not the back. God made you the head not the tail, so stand tall and take your place. When someone looks at you, even if you are having a day where you are feeling your weakest, remember your place and all that you have to offer to someone who has yet to learn what it means to be a leader.

No Matter What, Be Happy

Aren't there enough unhappy, miserable, complainers in the world? Don't be one. If people, places and things take you there, move! Perhaps start your day on someone's, anyone's or everybody's prayer line. If you really believe your God is great and can do all things, He can surely keep a smile on your face when you think of His goodness.

Family First

Never underestimate or forget the importance of the life of family and friends. Without them a piece of you gets snipped away and you're no longer whole.

As I walk this journey called life each day, I recognize that it's the love of others that continues to sustain me and the family and friends that I hold dear are what helps to make every day that much sweeter.

I Love Your Smile

There are days where even a smile from a stranger has brightened my day. Tomorrow look at someone you don't know and smile at them. They may not know you nor will they ever, but when they think of how jubilant that one smile from a stranger made them feel, they will remember the moment and the fact that you could have looked the other way, but you didn't. Imagine if because of that, they not only smiled all day, but they took the time to smile at someone else because they remembered how your smile made them feel. Smile for me!

Be Ready For Your Come Up

God spoke elevation and it is so. Be ready for those who don't understand or support your increase, but never look down on or step on someone who's trying to be where you are. You were once that person. Now that you have risen above, get ready for your blessing. It'll be even bigger when you share it with someone else who needs it.

Real Time Management

Multitasking is not taking twenty-four hours to do eight hours of work; it's getting twenty-four hours' worth of work done in eight hours.

Dance it Out

Every morning starts with a dance for me. Most mornings it's Whitney Houston's version of *I'm Every Woman*. That song empowers me and gets me out the door to the office.

Find a song that makes you feel like you can leap tall buildings in a single bound and dance it out especially if you need that extra push to deal with a day that may seem frustrating even before it starts. Go ahead, dance it out and see how much better you feel.

Be a Dream Chaser

Don't let your dream pass you by; that one oversight could be the difference between a dream coming to fruition and one only living in your mind while you sleep.

Let Ambition Free Your Mind

Instead of telling someone they are too ambitious, look in the mirror and tell yourself that you're not ambitious enough and then get up and move.

Momma's Rules Always Win

I've never tried my Momma and I never will. I don't care how old I am, she will always get my unconditional love and respect. Too many children are raised as an equal to their parents and when parents then try to correct the behavior, they don't understand why it's not working. As for my daughter, well for starters my crazy is not new to her so she knows better. (I'm saying this while sipping my tea)

I grew up at a time when you never, ever disrespected your mother and if she said jump, you asked her how high. I am making light of this here, but it's a serious circumstance. We have to do better when it comes to teaching our children to respect adult figures and it begins with what happens at home.

When your children don't respect you, they won't respect others and then we're raising a generation who don't care or fear anything.

A mother should be respected simply because her title is "Mother". Children who haven't learned that lesson need to be schooled immediately.

I am a mother first to my daughter and I make sure she understands what my role is in her life. I'm not a home-girl or a gal-pal, I am her mother and one of my tasks is to be sure she becomes a respectable member of society and that begins at home. It's not meant to be easy, but I hold on to my role as a mother and I demand respect. One day when she has her own children, she will understand, just as I learned from my own mother.

Thank goodness, my daughter knows better and she knows the value of respect. I love her for being the woman and daughter that she would want her own daughter to be to her.

Do It Today

I've decided that I shall live with a purpose today; tomorrow is not promised. It doesn't matter how many tomorrow's I see in my dreams, the only guarantee is right now. Do it!

The Power of One

Don't fear the path you may have to walk alone. There are times when you may be alone and feel lonely, but remember, if you have a problem with yourself in your down time, you can't expect someone else to bring you happiness.

My Brother's Keeper

Take standing in the gap seriously. We succeed when we help each other along. Be the keeper you would want someone to be for you in your time of need.

Just Like Glue

Appreciate those who stick around. People will come and go, but those who are meant to be a part of your life will stick around through thick and thin. Be thankful for the glue that has held you together.

An Uncloudy Day

My today looks good, despite everything that may cause a cloud. I look at that cloud and tell it to move out of my sky because there is a bright sunshine that's trying to get through to me.

Look Ahead

You hold the power to make your next step forward and not backward. There's nothing back there but history and it's the present and future that you want to focus on.

Don't Waste Your Talent

Your key to the empire is your talent; what are you doing with it? The gifts and talents that you possess could have been given to anyone so don't take it for granted that it was meant to be. Embrace it and let your light shine.

I Am My Sister's Keeper

Not all ladies are in competition with each other. There are those of us who just want to support and see another sister succeed. Be a woman who sees the potential in others even if their dreams don't line up with yours.

I support you, you support me and together we can kill the stigma that women can't get along and won't work together. I know we can.

Take a Stand

When do we as women begin to demand more respect? We need to stop allowing our own mistreatment by taking a stand against foolishness. We give into the image of what other people tell us we are supposed to be. We're better than that and rather than tell those naysayers, let's show them. We're in this together!

Change the Channel

There are some things and people that we should never give an audience to so that they can increase their following and platform of unconstructiveness.

When you're approached with negativity, pick up your imaginary remote control and point it at them while hitting buttons as if you're trying to change their mindset. They'll get the point.

Love Yourself

Don't let someone's opinion impact your grind. Not everyone will buy into the you you're trying to be. You have to know that you were created for greatness and that begins with knowing and loving who you are.

Leave Your Footprints in the Sand, Not On My Back

It's all good until you look back at the trail of hurt left behind. No one appreciates boot prints on their back, so tread lightly, cautiously and thoughtfully. The next time you fall, you don't want to get trampled because no one has your back.

I Know Who I Am

I know nothing about being insecure. My surety of who God created me to be overshadows that and forces me to walk in vastness.

One Moment in Time

I'm in love with life, not someone else's, but my own. It's lived one moment at a time and I don't take it for granted.

I don't live a life of what will be because any moment other than this very moment is not promised. I can dream a dream of many dreams and each may make me smile thinking of the possibilities, but living really is the here and now. Of course the life I've lived has a lot to do with the life I'm living.

When I stand in front of the mirror, what I see is the here and now and I smile. I smile because God could have had a different plan for my life.

I don't wonder what my life could have been if I were a star. I don't frown because I'm not a lottery winner sitting on piles of money ignoring family and friends who would wear me down with, "Cheryl, can you?"

I don't turn left or turn right and wonder how much more popular I would be if my body were that of someone who gets all of the attention.

I don't shed a tear or say "I wish" because that's not appreciating God for what He has done and that is giving me one moment at a time to be exactly who I am. I can look in the mirror and what I see is a woman who has lived a life that has had its ups and downs and because of those, I smile.

I look back over my life and see a young girl whose mother wanted her to know what it meant to have grace and poise so she enrolled her in the Wendy Ward Charm School. To this day I still remember what was taught to me about being lady-like.

I see a girl whose parents made great sacrifices and along with her brothers, were one of the first families to visit Walt Disney World in Florida when it opened.

I see a life lived that included vacations every first and second week of August as far back as I can remember. Those were times I hold very dear.

I see a person who was brought up in the church early in life and no matter what anyone else thinks they know about her, she has a relationship with God and He loves her in spite of any faltered steps.

I look at my reflection and I see many roads that have been traveled and some have left scars due to disappointment and loss of family and friends, but that reflection also shows that because of the one moment in time that God continues to grant, I am still here and with each moment comes a brand new me, a me I've never seen before and one that I will only see again when I look back on it.

I see a woman who has learned to embrace life and not live it according to admiration of the life others have, but thankful that the life I live has been blessed beyond measure. I have learned to not live my life according to the expectation of others and what they think I could, would or should do in order to say I'm living the American dream.

My life isn't based on what I can acquire for the future because it's not promised. What I can do is continue to live for today and give thanks that each breath is a blessing and I won't waste it.

I'm in love with life and that love is one moment at a time and when I again take a look at the reflection in the mirror, I'm smiling because finally I have learned to love who I am, I love what I see and I thank God for loving me. I won't let Him down by questioning anything He could have, would have or should have done. Instead, I smile and I say thank you for my right now because nothing else matters except this very second, this one moment in time.

I'm still a dreamer because that's hard to turn off, but I've learned to be happy in the moment and when the dream happens, I'll appreciate that moment too.

Dress For Success

Know when you've got the look. Not every look is for every situation or occasion. You have the power to turn people off or draw them in.

Be An Individual

I'm glad I've learned to do me and not the me someone else wants me to be. I've often run into situations where my personality is too strong for anyone to try and get me to follow the masses.

I recently had a conversation with someone who wanted me to have a drink. I declined as I always do because I don't drink alcohol. Then I was told that I didn't know how to have a good time because I didn't drink. My response was, I know how to have a good time without alcohol and it made me sad that he only knew how to have a good time when his speech was slurred from one too many.

I don't ask anyone to be like me or do the things I do. I say, do you and do what makes you happy, but don't knock how I choose to walk my own path and not one that is suggested for me. I know what's good for me and it is being me.

Time For Me

It's my time. I've compromised, I've sacrificed and now I'm looking to rediscover who I am to me.

I love doing things for other people, lending a helping hand where I can. When I realize I've done more for others than I've done for myself, I get that "me time" in even if it's sitting on my couch with my favorite bowl of peaches, music playing in the background, tablet on my lap, a book in my left hand and a remote control in my right while I'm watching re-runs of my favorite television shows; for that moment, it's all about me and it's heaven sent.

Be the Best You, You Can Be

Don't envy what you see; investigate so you know. What you see may look rosy because you're on the outside looking in. Unless you've walked their walk, you have no idea how they got what they have. Check it before you emulate it because what may not have caught them may snatch you right up. Knowledge could mean freedom.

Eyes Wide – Shut

What kind of a wake-up call do you need? Oftentimes we open ourselves up to people who are wolves in sheep's clothing. They come to kill and destroy all that you are meant to be because they see nothing in themselves when they look in the mirror. It's not enough that they are about nothing, but they get a thrill when they can pull you down to the nothingness of where they are.

I know some of us have a problem when it comes to walking away from someone when you think what you are experiencing is love. What if it's not love? Love isn't supposed to keep you in a dead space. Though your vision is clear and your eyes are wide open, when it comes to that wolf, your eyes are then, wide shut.

There are days when we have issues and we can't seem to get out of our own way. If that mountain that you're trying to climb over, that valley you're trying to get from down under or that river that no matter how hard you paddle, you can't seem to get across is a person standing in your way, hammer through that mountain, claw your way out of that valley and swim so hard and fast across that river people will think a shark is chasing you.

Push to get to a better place in your life where there is a bright side even if you are walking that walk alone. Your struggle to break free will be worth it when you realize, this time, it's not you in your way, but it's a person who adds no value to your life, who brings nothing to the table and who, even if given the chance, want nothing out of life. Why stay in that dead place with that spirit that has no vision, no drive and no determination to climb up to where you are. They want you to remain in that dead space with them because misery does want company. Love on yourself more and demand love, respect and a plan for coming up out of their place filled with nothingness before you accept them into your space.

Love is give and take, but if its only one-sided, you're wasting time in a life that's already too short, so make each moment count. You are better than that, you are more than that and you deserve everything in life that is good and fruitful, so go get your joy back.

When your eyes are no longer wide shut, you'll see that greater is within your reach when you drop that dead weight!

Show Problems the Door

Just when you think your problems are mountains, someone else's problems makes yours look like molehills. No matter how big or small, escort them to the door and never answer that knock again.

When You're Sick and Tired

It's okay to wash your hands of things that make you sick and tired. Sometimes it's just time to move on to something else, starting a new day with a new outlook on life and what you can do to be well and happy. Life is too short to not reach out and grab the happiness that's awaiting you especially when you realize you've spent too much time sacrificing for nothing at all.

Thank you God for moving me to another place and another level.

Time to Move

Sometimes we are our own worst enemy until we learn to get out of our own way. Feel free to kick yourself into motion when you look around for someone to blame for your current circumstance and you realize there is no one there because you are the cause.

Never Give Up

Do great things and go at it hard so you don't go home defeated. No one wants to walk away beaten and bruised feeling like you've lost all hope. Reach behind you and close that door while stepping up to the next door where once you walk through, you've just entered your brand new start.

A Piece of the Action

An empire doesn't build itself. It takes time and hard work. Never sit back and watch life happen, but get out there and get a piece of happiness for yourself.

An empire is not material things, but it's thinking and being bigger and greater than you ever thought possible. Get your plan in place, get up from where you've sat comfortably and make something happen. Everyone has to start someplace. The key to an empire is simply starting.

Mirror, Mirror

Loving the "me" that God sees! Don't expect anyone to see something wonderful and fantastic if you can't look in the mirror and say that about yourself. Let other's see the you as the great and awesome person you already know you are. Claim it!

Expect the Great

I don't live up to other's expectations; I have enough of my own to contend with daily. Sometimes people set low expectations for themselves but high expectations for you, knowing you're willing to spend a lifetime trying to match up. Set your own goals and be satisfied at your own achievements.

Keep Standing

Though others may fail you, never give up on yourself. Put more stock in what you can do for yourself than what you can do to try and please someone else. They may never be happy, but you will be because you know you've done your best. At times when your best isn't good enough for someone else, stand tall knowing your best is alright for you.

I Got You!

One woman empowering another leads to sisterhood. Women have to learn to come together by not finding fault in the women around them. No one has it all, but together we can create empires of strong women taking control and changing the minds and images of the young women who follow them. Make your next move knowing that a young sister is watching you.

Be Ready

God prepares me a little more each day for my next step up. My first step may have started at fear which then led to hope, but I press on because at the top I see the step that's labeled "Success".

I Like You; I Like Me

Don't just like; be likable. Don't expect that everyone will like you when all people hear is you complaining about what you don't like about yourself. Love you and all that makes you different.

A Mother's Work

I am here to help my daughter become a positive, productive woman in society. I want my daughter to be all that she can and wants to be and I make sure she knows that when she needs me, I am here to help guide her footsteps and to have her back. Times when she stumbles I will be here to reach down for her hand that's reaching up and out to me. I'm not a perfect mother and I don't do all things in a perfect way, but I'm thankful that God is a God of second chances because He's shown me how to be a mother of second, third and fourth chances.

I Want to Say Thank You

I am here to look out for my parents who sacrificed for me to have the life I'm now living. When I look back over my life, I know that I am blessed not just because God saw fit for my life to be wonderful and filled with love, but because He blessed me with parents who have loved me unconditionally and all they ask in return is that I appreciate and respect the life that I'm blessed to live. For that I am thankful and I give back to them the same unconditional love they've always shown me.

Say it With Your Chest

Why expect others to promote you when you
don't promote yourself? It's not ego, it's
confidence in your craft. Show as much love
for what you've created as you would like for
others to show for you.

A Brighter Tomorrow

Against any odds, stay the path. There are people who will never be happy or support anything you do, but that should not keep you from moving forward.

I have a dream and may not have all the skills I need to pull it off, but nothing will stop me from it even if some of the roads I take lead to nowhere. As long as I have the time and energy to go for it, I don't mind going back down a road already taken to try a different one. Eventually I'll find the road that leads to my dream fulfilled. I see myself in my future and I look good and it looks promising!

No One is Perfect

Stop expecting everyone to be perfect for your satisfaction. I'm happily flawed and I see each one as a learning experience for a better me in a new tomorrow.

Yes You Can, Can

Have a can-do attitude and watch it spread like wildflowers. You have it in you to succeed by telling yourself you can even when you feel like you can't. Go ahead and dance when you reap your reward.

Stay the Path

You'll never know unless you try. Days when obstacles seem so high that you can't get over them or so low that you can't get under them, try going around them or making a new path, always pushing your way through. Your destiny is on the other side and the hard work to get there will be well worth it.

Say What?

You have a voice and a choice. Use them so no one speaks and chooses for you. Don't let your silence be a sign of agreement when you know there is another option that works best for you. Speak up and be heard.

You Are My Friend

Hello happiness! You are my best friend and despite my trials and tribulations, if I know you're always there, I'm making my way to you, embracing you and basking in the feel of your love. Nothing compares to you and on those days when I try to do anything but find you, I appreciate that you never stop trying to rein me in.

Watch the Seed You Plant

Look to the positive and claim that bright side. Stop giving madness a moist place to grow and become infectious.

Know When to Turn Your Back

Don't become a casualty of other people's selfishness. Today's society is about get or get-got. Everyone is out for themselves and now more than ever, the need to respond to negativity in a negative way seems to be the norm. That only brings forth more negativity and no one wins. There are times when all you want to do is strike back when the right thing to do is to take the higher road and walk away. You are better than that and you were created for more than that.

When someone is on the attack, I find that as I've gotten older, it doesn't bother me as much as it did years ago. I know myself better than anyone and I know who I am, so I say continue to attack, but the love I have for myself lets me know you're not talking to me because the person you think you see and know is nothing compared to the awesome person I know I am.

Let adversity know that there is no space at the inn.

Two Way Street Called Respect

You want respect, then give it and earn it. Where has respect gone? No one seems to respect people, places or things anymore. Everyone seems to be on the defense from the start ready for a fight.

Even when it looks like you are fighting a losing battle, don't lose respect for the other person. Unless you have lived and walked in someone else's shoes, you don't know what their walk has been like, so try a little patience, tenderness, kindness and most of all respect.

Watch Your Step

Respect people's personal space or take responsibility for the outcome when you don't. When someone asks you to tread lightly, do it because they are entitled to have a space that includes only them.

Choose Your Words Wisely

Just because you have freedom of speech, doesn't mean you should, just because you can. I know an apology can go a long way towards healing a broken heart and spirit, but imagine how much hurt and anger could be avoided if you watched what you said, thought about it first then an apology wouldn't be needed and tempers wouldn't have to flair. I've learned when I have nothing good to say, I say nothing at all.

Some Things Aren't as Important

Every problem you make bigger seems miniature when you have a friend with a terminal illness.

A year ago I lost a good friend to cancer and through our friendship I watched her journey through her illness. If I never learn another lesson in my life, I learned that the here and now is what is important. It's time spent enjoying every moment given to me that's important.

She was a real trooper. There were days I knew she was in pain, but she carried on and did so with a smile on her face and a pep in her step. There were many ups and downs, but every conversation we had was always a good one. She would tell me of activities her kids were involved with or trips she was planning on taking and all of the other wonderful times she was enjoying spending with family and friends.

I admired her because her strength in keeping her head up knowing what she was going through made me ashamed of myself when I complained over small things. Through my friendship with her I realized I needed to give less attention to things that don't mean me any good and focus more on those things that are important.

One day she came over to me and asked me if I was still a big fan of the Ravens football team. I said yes and from behind her back she pulled out a black satin jewelry holder and gave it to me. She said someone had given it to her and now she was giving it to me. I opened it and inside were three handmade Baltimore Ravens beaded bracelets. She knew that I loved not only the team, but that style of bracelet. I appreciated the gesture and then she did as she usually did; she opened up my cabinet, pulled out my big bowl of candy and got her favorite fruit chews and walked off. That was two months before she eventually passed away and I cherish those three bracelets more than I cherish any other pieces of jewelry. I wear them occasionally, but mostly I keep them at home on my dresser in that same satin pouch that she gave them to me in. I don't know if her reasoning was to give me something to remember her by, but that's how I'd like to think of it.

After her passing there were many nice things said about her, but the greatest of those was her zest for life all the way to the end. She never felt sorry for herself, but she took the time to smell the roses and to make sure that those around her would be alright without her.

I'm thankful for the extra push I got from her to remember to appreciate every single second of every single day because the next moment isn't promised to anyone. In the blink of an eye life could change and you may not have the time left that you'd planned your whole life for, but a lifetime can be lived in a moment.

A moment can be as long or as short as you'd like it to be, but no matter the duration, don't waste it on foolish things or things that aren't worth the waste of time. A lot about my life changed the day she died and the greatest change was my appreciation for everything and I do mean everything.

Imagine all of the people who would love to still be here appreciating family and friends, but can't. Stand in the gap for them and embrace life. Live each day like it's your last.

The Circle of Love

Temptation happens even after you have a ring on it. Before you leap, think back to the reason why you fell in love. Think of the things that made you so happy that you either put the ring on or accepted the ring. Whatever those things were, get back to those moments and come back around to the love before the temptation and consider the risk. Some temptations feel good for a moment, but think of the loss that could result from a wrong decision. Good love given, is good love received; do both and choose happiness for an eternity.

Find Your Passion

I work for a living; my writing is a passion. Passions can make your life complete because it's not something you have to do, but something you love to do. I give just as much time to my wants and desires as I do to my needs and requirements.

Rise Above

I admire strong women who know how to rise above without trying to damage another person's character.

We have all been hurt before and we remember how that felt. Use that pain of that hurt before you lash out and remember you are better than that. Do better when you know you can.

Friendship Has Limits

Don't aid in your friend's pity parties; it doesn't benefit them and you help keep them bound.

Aim High

Set high standards for those around you and those in positions of authority. We have to change a generation that's coming along feeling entitled. Achievement happens with hard work and education not by handouts.

Keep Your Chin Up

Be positive today and don't let anyone take you to a negative space. That space is filled with misery, discontent and disappointment and you want to live and breathe in an environment rich with love, happiness and bliss.

Yesterday is Gone

Leave your past behind you; your future is too bright to keep looking backward. Carry good memories into your present and smile when you think on how far you've come. Some didn't make it this far, so be thankful you have a God of new chances birthed every day.

Don't Be A Fool Again

I have learned to forgive, but never forget. Fool me once, shame on you; fool me twice, shame on me.

We've all played the fool a time or two, being the giver and receiver of foolishness. Childish ways should remain in your childhood and as an adult, it's time to take the blinders off, look around and vow that you will only accept better because you deserve it.

I'm Still Me

I'm not defined by the company I keep. God defined me before I was born and I'm following that path.

I've made many changes in my life over the years, some good and some not so good.

I may have aged, I may have grown, I know I have more zest for life though my level of energy has decreased.

I know my walk is different and certainly my talk is.

My strength makes me believe I can do anything.

My surroundings have changed and my lifestyle has improved.

I've gotten older and learned what real

friendship is and for those who freely give it from the heart, I thank you.

I see more gray hair and the extra pounds are unmistakable and I smile knowing it's all a part of who I am and that's fine by me.

I demand more and I give much more.

My heart is bigger and my love is greater.

My circle is smaller, yet my confidence in those around me grows more and more.

I laugh harder and I play even harder.

I sacrifice my time for those I love and I don't waste it on those who look down on me.

I've lost loved ones over the years and at that time I couldn't imagine life without them, but I'm still here and I'm thankful that my memories keep me in touch with who they were.

I've had my struggles as a parent and believe

that troubles don't last always.

I'm a living testimony that there is a bright side when at one time things seemed dark with no way out.

I have many material things, but they don't and can't replace the sound of my parents' voices. They are more precious than any gold!

I used to look over my life and think of what I wish I had done differently, but as I've gotten older, I've come to realize that if I could have made a change, perhaps something or someone I have in my life right now wouldn't be here and knowing that, I wouldn't change a thing.

Despite any ups or downs, after forty-nine years of being alive and free, I am still me and for that that, everything in my life has been worth this very moment.

These Feet Were Made For Walking

I walked in my new season today. I put faith in who and what I was created to be and I kept walking and didn't look back. I have no clue of what the future may hold for me because all I know is what I see right now. What I want to be is within me and it began when I learned to walk and not crawl. I may not get there when other's do, but when I do get there, it will be just in time.

Letting God Lead

In spite of it all, God is still in control and I wouldn't have it any other way.

What Defines You

I am not my failures, but I have used them to stand on to get to my new empire state of mind.

Failing does not permanently cripple me against ever getting back up and trying again. I choose to let my fight define me and not the fact that I once fell.

Don't let mistakes keep you from seeing what you can be. When you rise and stand tall, the definition of you will be "overcomer".

Keeping Promises

Never give up on the promises you've made to yourself.

I promise to love me first, because until I do, I can't fully love another person.

I promise to never give up because the other side could be the key to my kingdom.

I promise to smile through the pain when I know trouble doesn't last always.

I promise to trust God knowing I am His and what He has ordained for my life, I boldly walk into.

I promise to give thanks in everything knowing everything good or bad could be worse.

I promise to give myself a break from living up to the ideas and plans others have for my life. We all have to walk a path and be responsible for the outcome.

I promise to keep the promises I've made for myself and learn to be a better me.

The Struggle is Real

The struggle will make you stronger because the best is yet to come. Throughout life, there will be many struggles, but what matters most is your response to them.

I Hear You Momma

Because of my mom, nothing keeps me down.
She taught me to press my way through.

Keep it to Yourself

Your secret is no longer a secret the minute you tell it to someone. No matter how you phrase "don't tell anyone", it stopped being a secret as soon as it left your lips. Don't be upset when a friend shares your secret with someone else because if you really wanted it to be a secret, you wouldn't tell anyone. The only way to secure a secret is to take it to the grave. At that time, it truly is a well-kept secret.

The World is Yours

Expand your horizons and listen to something other than what you always listen to. There is so much more to life than that box you're in. When you peep out over the edge of it, there is more to what you see than meets the eye. Go explore!

All Things New

Your clean slate happened the moment you opened your eyes today, so make it great. There are some people who made choices in their lives and have problems that waking up and seeing the bright sunshine just won't fix. When you have the ability to freely walk the streets and go where you like, embrace that life and everything that comes along with it. Not everyone can enjoy such pleasures because though it's a new day, they won't have the experience of new things. Leave the old for the history books and write a new story as if each day is a new beginning.

Nothing But Net

I was born to win, created to succeed and I live to achieve. I see every action as an attempt at playing a game of basketball. My purpose is not just to make it in the basket, but to make the ball go in without hitting the rim. As I'm traveling down the court, there is constant dribbling and making my way through opponents whose objective is to stop me. Not only do I want to make the basket and win, but I want to make it so that there is no doubt that I was born for this. I want all of my effort to show the work I've put in and when that ball hits nothing but net, the crowd will cheer, my opponents will know my confidence of knowing I could do it and I'll pat my own self on the back and say great job.

Approach every task with the goal of hitting nothing but nets. Go for the gusto and don't just be mediocre; be the best.

Dreams are Worth the Work

When all is said and done, I wrote a book and I feel good about that. I don't consider myself a perfect writer and in everything, there is room for improvement.

When I started this journey working on my first novel, which was a romance novel, I had no idea I'd still be writing novels two years later. My first novel called *Bachelor Not For Sale,* started out as a class project for a Creative Writing class. The enjoyment on the faces and the accolades from my fellow classmates was inspiring. I didn't know that I could do it and one day I decided to sit down and turn my project into a novel. Months later that novel was released and it was embraced with open arms.

I didn't know I had a dream to write until I'd actually done so and now I can't imagine not writing. This journey has been both rewarding and therapeutic. Nothing could have prepared me for the excitement I feel every time I complete a new novel or get an idea for a new one. What I can say is a dream fulfilled is a dream well worth the work and the wait. I went back a year later and released another edition of that first novel to improve the writing and make some corrections of things I've learned over that first year. I'd never written anything like that before and now two years in, I've learned a lot and I take my writing very serious.

The one dream of getting my first novel out has led to other dreams that I'm currently working on. It was easy to begin working on a new dream after realizing the sense of satisfaction I got after I accomplished the first one. Now I'm on to bigger and better because I see greater. I already know it will be worth it because I didn't sit on it. I'm doing something about it.

Stay on Top

Stop listening to and going by what people say who do nothing but criticize and have nothing going on for themselves. Want more for yourself than what a dream-killer wants. They don't see what you see and they never will so their opinions don't matter.

My Cup Runneth Over

Many days I find more on my plate than I can possibly take care of within a day. There is no one to blame but me for allowing myself to get so overwhelmed. I've learned to backtrack, discover what's the least important by setting priorities and then giving myself time to relax in between tasks. What works best for me is finding time for myself in the midst of a life overwhelmed with things to do. After a much needed rest, things begin to look a lot better as long as I learn to pour in as much as I pour out.

True Friendship

Sometimes you have to realize someone you have been calling a friend really isn't. They are just someone who should be placed in the category of someone you happen to know.

Glass Half Full

I no longer say, "Why me?" I'm now declaring, "Why NOT me!

Be Your Biggest Supporter

When no one applauds, clap for yourself. You'll be surprised at how clapping for yourself can sound like a stadium full of people cheering you on.

If no one else celebrates you, celebrate yourself because you and only you will know what it took to get where you are.

Be About Something or Exit Stage Left

There are things and people I am simply no longer giving attention to. It's not a resolution; it's just a fact.

Go From Best to Better

If everyone treated the next person better, we'd all be better at being better people.

What Matters to You

All lives matter and when we learn to respect each other, it will no longer be an issue.

So much has been in the media lately about whether or not lives matter and the answer is that every life should matter. One life is just as precious as the next so the next time you see someone and you think because of how they dress or behave makes them a person who doesn't matter to you, imagine yourself on your worse day and remember you could be one paycheck away from being the same person you looked down on.

Second Chances

Don't give someone a second chance to hurt you, but give them a second chance to get it right.

Take One For the Team

There is a personality that doesn't lend itself to always being a team player. It's the kind of person who feels if there is a job to be done, they could do it better themselves rather than spread the responsibility around to others to do.

I've been guilty of that because there are times when I know I could complete a task correctly instead of leaving it to a member of a team to do it and do it wrong. I had to learn that sometimes as a member of a team, it's okay to be a part of a mistake. The bigger and better woman in me has learned to stay a part of the team and be a part of the mistake. As a part of a team, I've learned to then go back to the drawing board and correct the mistake together. Teamwork is often the key to success especially after a failure. There is no need to be an island.

Faith, Hope and Love

Keep the faith and know that your life is not lived in vain, but in prosperity and fortune. That fortune may not be full of monetary riches, but think of all of the lives that have been enriched because you lived.

Hope keeps you looking for the next moment when you can change what was bad into something that's great. Hope should make your heart beat faster, your steps quicken and it should give you some insight into an opportunity for a better day.

Love others the way you want to be loved and facilitate a change in a heart that's hurting.

The Power of Yes

There are days when I wish I could strike the word "No" from the dictionary. It's a strong word and it can overpower a can-do mindset. Even though we are forced to utter the occasional "No", always say yes to yourself. I may not be able to remove the word from the dictionary, but I can remove it from my vocabulary. I vow to use the power of "Yes" to force my next step. I've already agreed to it so there is no backing down after that. That yes can lead to mighty big things and I'm ready.

Respect Your Own Grind

Do it like no one is watching or cares. When we look for approval from others, we don't get the satisfaction we would get if we made moves just to satisfy ourselves. If someone else doesn't approve, press on and don't worry about impressing others. Life is too short to not be happy for yourself.

That Moment When....

That moment when you realize people aren't perfect, but some are just perfect for you.

That moment when you envied a friend's life until you find them crying because their perfect life on the outside is actually miserable on the inside.

That moment when you're a few days late and a dollar short and you go to get your clothes from the dryer and find a five dollar bill.

That moment when you survive an accident and you read stories of other's who had the same type of encounter and didn't survive.

That moment when the doctor says there is no hope, but God says hope is what He does best.

That moment when you know you don't qualify for the position, but you get the call that the job is yours.

That moment when you've lost someone close to you and you turn on the radio and their favorite song is playing.

That moment when you question whether your child will understand all that you've tried to do and the day comes when you realize, they got it.

That moment when you are secretly going through something and your mother calls to say she had a feeling you needed her and your world is right again.

The moment when you thought someone would be in your corner only to find they didn't have much of a positive impact in the first place.

For every moment you think you won't survive, God sends a lifeline to show you that He will provide a ram in the bush.

Having Power Doesn't Make You Powerful

Having power over someone can go to your head quickly. Before you try to wield that power in a way that intimidates another person, put yourself in their shoes and consider how you'd like to be treated. From that vantage point you'll realize that someone may have power, but it doesn't make them powerful. It means they have the ability to make or break a spirit so think before you use the power you have over someone.

Dance to the Music

Music can free the mind from the clutter of a busy day. Put on your favorite beat and tune out the world while you find your peace. Give into the feeling of tapping your feet or snapping your fingers and see how fast a wave of enjoyment can overtake a crazy day.

Disconnect From the Matrix

Find time daily to shut off all electronics and get back to the basics of reading a book or having a face to face conversation with someone. Electric devices are nice and convenient, but they take us away from actual human contact.

Situational Awareness

Stay alert and be mindful of what could happen based on what you see. A situation or person could appear to be harmless and when you get comfortable and let your guard down, you may become too vulnerable to what someone else has planned for you. You may not be able to control every situation, but knowing what is for you is a good start to an outcome that will benefit you and not harm you.

I Know I Belong

I never doubt that I matter. We're a world full of people who want to control when and where everyone else belongs. I've been to places where I immediately know it's not a place for me and I turn around and go in the opposite direction. That wasn't always the case and I've learned some good lessons in life. I've learned to watch the people and things I surround myself with and I make sure they are for my good. There is a perfect place for me even if in that space, there is only me. I can be who I want to be without putting on a façade. I can let my hair down and not worry if I will be critiqued. I can pick and scratch and not offend another person. This place sounds a lot like home and home is where I know I belong even if I'm not welcomed anyplace else. Sometimes, there's no place like home.

Plant, Harvest and Reap

An idea is a powerful thought. It can start out as something as small as a mustard seed that can grow into something as tall as the highest mountain top and as wide as the sea. Think of what could happen if that idea came and went and you did nothing about it. It would dry up and scatter like the dust on the ground. Now think of the creation you could make if you took that idea and planted it.

Planting would consist of taking that idea and thinking of the plan to make it grow. Think about all of the things you would need in order to turn that idea into something real. You may have to work hard at it, but it's doable. To begin, see that idea for what it could be when it is complete and work the plan to get there. Now that you have the idea deeply rooted and planted in your mind, it's now time to harvest it.

During the harvesting the objective is to make it grow. Gather the resources you'll need and outline the path you need to take when the idea is ready to be birthed. Every time you feed the idea with ways to succeed, you're harvesting it until it's time for it to become a reality. There may be days where there's a drought and you can't think of anything else to feed it and on those days, take a rest. Every good idea needs a time of reassessing to be sure you have everything in place for that magical day when your idea comes alive. There may be some days when you're harvesting in a monsoon and things may seem overwhelming. Don't worry about doing too much because in the end, the extra could be exactly what your idea needed. Once your plan is in place and you've worked on the idea to the point that it's ready to be birthed, stand back and watch in awe as something that seemed too small for you to see is now life-changing. This is where you reap the harvest from what you planted.

You will feel a great sense of accomplishment when the small idea you started planting has grown because you harvested and nourished it and never gave up on it. Take pride in patting yourself on the back because where others may have given up, you hung in there and now you know what it feels like to experience greater.

It's Okay to Cry

Crying can be healing and shouldn't be known as something sad. Today I thought about my brother who passed away five years ago and I cried thinking of all of the things he didn't get a chance to see and do. I cried because even though I didn't see or talk to him every day, I could if I wanted to and now that's not possible. I've had some wonderful moments in my life that I know he'd be patting me on the back and saying, good job. There are days like today where the cries wrack my body and even in that, I realized I needed that cry. I needed to get it out in order to move forward.

Take Pride in What You Do

What you do will have meaning and purpose. It may not suit everyone, but someone, even one person will find what you do helpful and inspiring. That person watching you wondering if you will make it may be the next success story all because of you. It's a heavy burden, but you can handle it because you were made to do it.

It's Like Baking a Cake

First you shop for everything you need. You bring it home and set everything out, taking stock to be sure you haven't left anything out. You then begin adding each ingredient to your bowl one at a time. You check the box to be sure you've added everything because any missing ingredient means it won't come out the way you want. Now you start mixing and you mix everything up until it appears smooth and creamy making sure there are no lumps. You then measure your portions out perfectly before placing it in the oven at the right temperature setting the timer for the correct amount of time so that you don't undercook it or overcook it. Once it's done, you take it out and add the icing that will turn it into a masterpiece. Once you bite into it, you realize it was well worth the shopping, the mixing, the baking and the dressing it up in the end. That's how you should approach every task in life.

Before you tackle anything, make sure you have everything you need before you start. Make a list so that you don't leave anything out. That list could consist of setting aside the time needed, gathering financial resources and of course every idea you have that will pull it all together. When you have everything, get a vision board set up and bring all of your ingredients to the table. Write out your game plan and follow your own directions to be sure you come to a successful end. Pull it all together by combining your resources and your ideas to make the perfect mix. Sometimes, at this point you may have to step away from it to be sure you've done all you need to do. Let the plan bake and simmer for a while. In the end it will all come together because you had the right ingredients and you planned it out well. When it's done, you can dress it up and make it all pretty and presentable. The joy you'll feel from the accomplishment will be worth it just as it is the moment you cut a slice into a cake and take that first bite and find that it's just right. Get baking!

Living on Top Of The World

My place up high doesn't mean I'm looking down on anyone. It means I look down and realize how far I've come from where I first started.

I had little back then, but I had determination.

I spoke up very little before, but now I walk with a permanent bullhorn plastered to my lips.

I hid in the shadows before, but now I enjoy the sun that's at my back casting a glow on all that I am.

I live on top of my world because under me is the struggle and I was allowed to see this day and all that I've accomplished and the view from the top looks spectacular. I call it Blessed!

Listen Up!

Can you hear me? What about now? Am I talking loud enough? All I want to say is someone is counting on you today to make a difference in your life so that they can believe the same can happen for them.

Make it Work

Not every situation is a prime situation for reaching a goal. Sometimes a good start may lead to a failure, but remember to always start again.

We often work around people with personalities that don't connect with our own. We have friends who aren't really friends based on the definition of the word, but they are people we've encountered and have kept communicating with. We all sometimes take actions we do out of need as opposed to doing so because we want to. Not everything in life will be exactly what we want it to be, but if we stay at it, we can still make it work out for our good. Find the good in any situation and focus on that to get you through.

.

In Everything, Give Thanks

When all is said and done, be thankful that the sun came up another day for you. Maybe the day won't turn out exactly the way you expected, but realize with as rough as it may turn out to be, it could be the last day the sun rises for you, so make it count. Don't miss a chance to be thankful just because.

Enjoy this short story that was a part of the inspirational book, One Sister Away: Encouraging Words From One Sister to Another

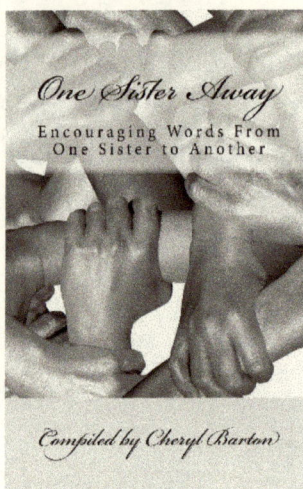

Who Are They – A Short Story
By Cheryl Barton

"Tracee, are you ready to go?"

Kortney looked at her best friend with a face full of frustration at the length of time it was taking her to get dressed.

"Kortney I'm going as fast as I can. You know I have to have the perfect look. I can't go out looking any kind of way."

"We're only going to the mall to shop for school clothes. What's the big deal?"

Kortney didn't understand the change in her best friend. They have been best friends since elementary school and now they were both entering high school together and excited about the upcoming first day of school. The biggest excitement around a new school year was going shopping for school clothes. They were happy that they were attending a school that didn't have a specific dress code which also meant they both needed to be dressed in the latest gear if they wanted to be noticed. At least that's what Tracee told her. She had different ideas on learning to be just who she was without trying to impress other people.

Kortney watched as her best friend threw one outfit after the other across the bed.

"The big deal is that we may run into some of the kids from the school and then on the first day they could recognize me from being dressed down and I'll live with that stigma forever."

"Tracee, you are way too concerned about what everyone else thinks, especially about what you have on. Don't you know there are kids our age who have one outfit to wear every day and are happy they have that? You have two closets full of stuff and your biggest concern is if someone else likes what they see you in."

"Stop acting like the way you dress doesn't matter to you Kortney. You know what they say! You're only a part of the in-crowd when you wear what everyone else is wearing as far as the top fashion for the season."

"Really Tracee? Who are they?"

Tracee stopped going through her clothes and turned toward Kortney.

"Why are you acting all crazy Kortney? Why are you getting an attitude about clothes?"

"I'm not getting an attitude. I'm simply

asking you who they are."

"What?" Tracee said looking perplexed.

"Every time you talk about fashion or make-up you always say 'they say' and I want to know who they are."

"Girl you know. They are the people who write fashion columns and they are those people who tell you what is and is not hot. They set the tone and the standard for fashion and style and if you don't follow them then you're nobody."

"So I'm a nobody if I don't let someone I don't know, someone who doesn't define who I am and someone who doesn't pay for anything that I have, tell me how to dress? So you live your life according to these 'they' people?"

"Kortney stop making this into something bigger than it is. All I'm saying is I take pride in how I look and that way I won't end up being the person having fingers pointed at me and being snickered at and I'll always be a part of the "it" crowd because I'm always fly! Girl, we are nothing if we are not trending when it comes to fashion and style. Without that we are just nothing."

Kortney decided to let the conversation go

because clearly they were not on the same page when it came to how important what they looked like to others was. She felt it was time Tracee got a lesson in how clothes don't make the person and she had the perfect way to prove it to her.

"Hey Tracee, before we go to the mall I need to make a quick stop at the library first."

"Okay, sure. Let's go."

Tracee followed Kortney into the library and up to the second level where a young woman sat alone in a quiet corner studying. She watched as Kortney walked right up to her.

"Hey Carmen!" Kortney said.

"Hey Kortney. What are you doing here? I was expecting your brother. Did he send you to tell me he wasn't coming?"

"No. He told me you would be here and I wanted to stop in and say hi while you were in town. This is my friend Tracee."

Tracee looked at Kortney's friend and wondered who she was. She gave Carmen a once over and noticed her clothes were from at least ten years ago. Her tennis were no names and so were her jeans. Her top was a plain white shirt and her face had no make-up besides a little lip gloss. Even though she was clearly very pretty lots of make-up was the trend these days and clearly this girl didn't have it. Though her hair was neat it didn't have a lot of style to it and her nails didn't even have any polish on them. Who was this plain Jane, Tracee thought?

"Tracee, this is Carmen a friend of my brother's."

She knew it would be rude to not speak so she uttered a light hello.

"Hello Carmen."

"Hi Tracee," Carmen said. "Nice to meet you. You look very nice. Where are you girls heading out to a party or something?"

"No, we're just going to the mall."

"Are you coming along with us Carmen? I'm sure you could probably pick up a few nice things?" Tracee said with judgment in her voice.

Kortney was glad Carmen didn't pick up on how snide Tracee was trying to be, but she knew Tracee's lesson would soon come.

"No I have some studying to do."

"On a Friday? Who studies on a Friday?"

"I do if I plan to make something of myself

one day. Education is important. How are your grades?" Carmen asked Tracee.

Kortney stood back and watched the scene play out.

"Oh my grades are okay. Of course, I'm planning to be in the fashion industry, so I'm not all that worried about school. I have to be sure I look the part more than I need to act the part, if you know what I mean."

"Not really, but humor me. I see you are laced in the finest fashion right now, especially for a trip to the mall, but I'm not hating. You look very nice, but you'll need to do more than just look nice even in the fashion world."

"Well some people do books and I do looks and I'm not hating either, if you catch my drift."

Kortney smiled at all the shade that was being thrown, but she didn't intervene. She knew Carmen had this.

"Oh, yes I catch it with no problem. I admire your style, but style isn't everything and it shouldn't make you who you are or who you plan to be. Isn't there more to you than just what you have on?"

"In this day and age, what you look like is

everything. You have to have the long, tight weave like mine, the coke-bottle figure, a behind that you can rest a quarter on and it won't fall off and your gear has to be top of the line. What good is all that education if no one wants to be friends with you or even be around you because you don't fit the mold of what society says you should look like?"

Kortney then chimed in.

"Carmen, my friend Tracee here has the "they" mentality where it doesn't matter what she thinks of herself, it only matters what others think of her, especially of what she has on. In her mind she is nothing if she isn't turning heads when she walks into a room."

"Is that so?" Carmen asked.

Tracee turned to Kortney with a look that said she wasn't happy with being put on the spot.

"Kortney is exaggerating, but yes I like to stay with the latest fashions and I think it's a big part of who you are and who you'll become."

"So you're saying I'm not somebody important if I don't have labels on everything I wear?"

"I'm not saying that about you, I'm only talking about me here."

"So, you didn't take a good, long look at me when you came in and judged me?" Carmen asked.

Tracee said nothing. She wondered how this outing to the library turned around to be about her.

"I'm just saying that you're sitting here in a library on a Friday afternoon studying by yourself and I don't see any friends around. Clearly you didn't really care much about who saw you because you have on the plainest clothes I've ever seen on a female. Not judging, but you look like you didn't really care what you put on when you left your house. I'm not throwing shade or anything; I'm just saying you can catch more bees with honey."

"Who says I'm trying to catch anything?"

Tracee started to feel bad. She didn't know how the conversation had taken such a terrible turn.

"I'm sorry Carmen. I'm really not judging you. I'm just explaining me."

"Tracee, I know you don't mean any harm and if you're paying attention, I'm not upset at all. I'm actually enjoying this conversation with you. I come across young ladies all the time who think just as you do. I don't consider them all as judgmental, though some are, but I don't think every book should be judged by its cover. I think the important parts are what's in between the pages of the book. I respect that you love to be beautiful and fly at all times. There is nothing wrong with that, but make sure you don't think that's all you are. Don't live by the standards someone set in a magazine, but be the standard by recognizing who you are, with or without the hottest fashions. I could drip myself in the greatest fashions, but I'm more concerned about why would I want to base who I am on what I see in a magazine or read in a column. Just make sure, again, that's not all you see in yourself because you are more than that."

"Tracee is good people Carmen. She just doesn't think far beyond her closet."

"Sure I do Kortney. There you go exaggerating again."

"Really Tracee? We are going to the mall and you have on four inch heels. Who does that and why?"

"These are the latest Manolo's girl! I wouldn't be seen in anything but the best."

"Is that your best Tracee? Your outward appearance? What about what's inside?"

"They don't see or care about what's inside. It's all about what they see when they first look at you."

"Who are they?" Carmen asked.

Kortney looked at Tracee and smiled.

"I asked her the same question. She has these mysterious 'they' people who are the authors and finishers of her life. She bases what she wears everyday on this mysterious group of people."

Tracee looked embarrassed. Why was she being harassed simply because she liked to look nice?

"What is this, pick on Tracee day?"

"Not at all Tracee. I think Kortney brought you by here to meet me for a reason."

"Why would she do that?"

"I think it's to prove to you that there is more to someone than meets the eye."

"Okay, game over. Somebody tell me what's going on here," Tracee exclaimed.

"First, tell me what was your first thought

when you saw me," Carmen asked.

"Okay, I'll play along. I always look a person over when I meet them, so I saw that your gear is all plain, nothing special. I don't see any make-up and though your hair is nice, you could really hook it up if you added a weave and a nice cut to it."

"I would do that why? If you haven't noticed, my hair is long and full already. Why would I weave it up?" Carmen asked.

"I know. I'm just saying weaves are the thing these days. You never know who you could meet. You could meet the man of your dreams and he could be rich and famous and sweep you off of your feet and take you away where you'd never have to worry about studying again because he'd take care of you. He wouldn't notice you dressed like that. There are fashion magazines for a reason and they all say you are what you look like."

"There's that mysterious 'they' again," Kortney said.

"Stop it Kortney. It's what all the latest fashion magazines say, so it must be true."

"Tracee, there is nothing wrong with fashion as long as you know that's not the most important thing in life. At your age, make sure you focus on your education as well and don't worry so much about what others think about how you look. When you don't meet their high standards, you'll fall so fast you won't know how to pick yourself back up because you were so dependent upon what someone else thought of how you looked. I could tell when you first walked up to me that the first thing you did was judge me by what I had on. I'm not mad about it."

"So now who are you and why did Kortney bring me here to meet you."

"My name is Carmen, yes, but it's not the name you would recognize. My middle name is Carmen. My first name is Arianna."

Nothing rang a bell to Tracee so she looked to Kortney for help.

"Tracee, what's the name of the biggest fashion magazine around?"

"That's easy, it's On Top Magazine". That's the number one fashion magazine in the world. Why?"

Kortney and Carmen both smiled while Tracee continued to look bewildered.

"Tracee, her name is Arianna Mazé. Her

father owns On Top Magazine and the fashion line to most of the clothes in your closet!"

"What!!!!!"

Tracee stared at Carmen, bewildered.

"Lies! I don't believe it! Stop playing around with me Kortney. What would his daughter Arianna be doing sitting here in the library dressed like this studying?"

"Carmen, show her," Kortney said.

Carmen reached in her bag, pulled out one of the On Top magazines and sure enough, inside staring back at her was a very glammed up picture of Carmen with the caption that read, 'Orin Mazé and his daughter, Arianna at fashion week.' There was no way to mistake that the girl in the picture was in fact Carmen.

"Oh my goodness. It is you. I don't understand. Why are you here, in a library studying and how do you know Kortney."

Kortney smiled like the cat had her tongue.

"Kortney you've been holding out on me. What gives?"

"Let me answer first," Carmen said. "I love fashion and I, of course love my dad and my family and I could have anything in the world I want, but what I want most is my law degree. I grew up wearing everything that was top of the line, but it didn't make me happy as some people may think it would. I wanted to be more than just pictures on and in magazines. It took me a few years to get away from the person you see in that picture and to become the person you see sitting here much happier. My family is part of the 'they' that you keep referring to and believe me, we don't even believe the stuff we write about. It's done to sell fashion and to sell magazines. This, what you see in this magazine, is all for show. I could be glammed up and walk around in the finest, but I choose not to because for once in my life, I want to be taken seriously for who I am in between the pages and not just the cover."

Tracee now understood. She was spending all of her time focusing on what she looked like and not really on who she was. Clothes didn't really tell you anything about a person because clearly she misread who Carmen was.

"I'm sorry for judging you by your clothes."

"It's okay Tracee. Just make sure you care just as much about the inside as you do about the outside."

"Okay, one question has been answered, but

I have another. How do you know Kortney?"

Kortney chimed in the answer.

"She's dating my brother. They met in law school and have been dating for about a year. She's in town for a few days to visit him while they both prepare to take the bar exam. My brother swore us all to secrecy. They're engaged to be married now so I asked Carmen if it was okay if I introduced you and she agreed. I just wanted you to see that the outside doesn't tell you a lot about who a person is. You have always been so hooked on who you are on the outside that I wanted to you finally see you can be and are much more than that. You know how plain my brother is and look who he snagged!"

"She's right Tracee. You are much, much more and believe me the 'they' do what they do to make money, not necessarily because it's the gospel. Take it for what it is, but don't make it who you are. The 'they don't know you, but in order for them to stay relevant, they have to have a way to continually draw you in. Be you and get that education. Let your Mr. Right get to know who you are and not just what you look like. I looked just like this when her brother and I met and we fell in love with who we are on the inside. It took him months to find out who I was and that was because I told him. At that point I had to because we wanted the families to meet."

"Well this has been enlightening. Never judge a book by its cover couldn't be any truer than it is right now."

"That's good to know. Well I don't want to keep you ladies from the mall. Have fun shopping and Kortney, bring her by the hotel tomorrow before I leave and we can all do lunch."

"I will," Kortney replied.

Tracee smiled, relieved at how the conversation turned into a lesson learned for her.

"First, though, we're going back to my house so that I can put on some shoes that I can comfortably shop in," Tracee added before following Kortney out.

As they left the library, Tracee turned to Kortney.

"I've been acting a little crazy about outer appearance lately haven't I?"

"Yeah you have and you made more than a

few mentions of 'they' like it was all you depended on for who you are and I knew differently."

"Well, no more 'they' for me. Who are they anyway? I'm more about me and what's in between the pages and not just my cover."

**

This story and more can be found in, *One Sister Away: Encouraging Words From One Sister to Another*, a compilation project birthed from the heart and spirit of Author Cheryl Barton, bringing together sisters from all walks of life to inspire and encourage another sister.

One Sister Away is filled with poetry, short stories, life-lessons, testimonies and short passages of encouragement.

Get your copy of this inspirational novel at www.bartonpublishingLLC.com in paperback and for your electronic device.

Look for Volume 2 of, *One Sister Away: Encouraging Words From One Sister to Another*, available Summer 2015 at <u>www.bartonpublishingLLC.com</u>.

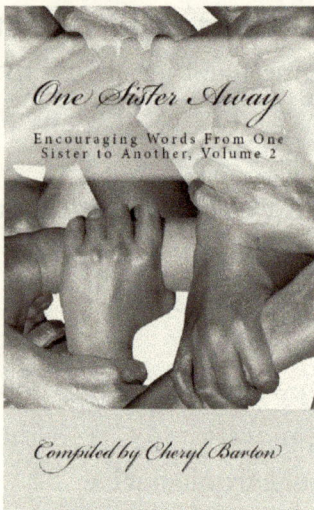

One Sister Away

Encouraging Words From One
Sister to Another, Volume 2

Compiled by Cheryl Barton

ABOUT THE AUTHOR

Cheryl Barton is an author who was born and raised in Baltimore, Maryland, where she works full-time and writes novels during her free time. .

As a romance novelist, Cheryl released her first novel, 'Bachelor Not for Sale' in April 2013. Following this release, she has authored nine additional novels, including two follow-ups to 'Bachelor Not for Sale', 'A Designed Affair' and 'A Perfect Combination'. She also released 'The Artist', 'The Bookkeeper', 'The Chef' and 'The Dancer', the first four in a new twenty-six, Amorous Occupations book series. She also released a holiday short story, 'Holly for Christmas', a Valentine Novella, 'Second Chances' and combining romance with inspiration, she released 'Down, But Not Out: Breaking Chains' in mid-2014.

For more information on these and new novel releases, you can visit her website at www.cherylbarton.net.

Cheryl is the owner of Barton Publishing, LLC, a media publishing company and is excited about book projects from new writers under her publishing label. Visit the publishing company website at www.bartonpublishingLLC.com.

Cheryl is the Founder and Executive Director

of Sisters About Making Moves, Inc., (SAMM) a non-profit organization whose mission is to educate, embrace and empower sisterhood within the community. SAMM is doing their part in the community and has championed a toiletry drive for the House of Ruth of Maryland and for the city's homeless community through their Blessing Bags which are bags filled with necessary toiletries.

Cheryl is also a member of the Black Writers' Guild of Maryland.

Connect with the Author:

Website: www.cherylbarton.net
Facebook: Author Cheryl Barton
Twitter: Author Cheryl Barton
Instagram: Author Cheryl Barton
Email: cheryl@cherylbarton.net

9780692418321